Language Being Time

ALSO BY JOHN PHILLIPS

Language Is (Sardines Press, San Francisco, CA, 2005)
What Shape Sound (Skysill Press, Nottingham, 2011)
Heretic (Longhouse, Guilford, VT, 2016)
Shape of Faith (Shearsman Books, Bristol, 2017)

CHAPBOOKS

Instances (with Roger Snell) (Third Ear Books, 2000)
While (Longhouse, 2000)
Path (Longhouse, 2002)
A Small Window (Longhouse, 2005)
Soundless (Punch Press, 2007)
Pages (Country Valley Press, 2008)
Spell (Kater Murr's Press, 2009)
Fault (Kater Murr's Press, 2013)
This (Smallminded Books, 2016)
No Preference (Longhouse, 2018)
Hourglass (Longhouse, 2020)
Prague, etc. (Kater Murr's Press, 2021)

John Phillips

LANGUAGE BEING TIME

Shearsman Books

First published in the United Kingdom in 2024 by
Shearsman Books Ltd
PO Box 4239
Swindon
SN3 9FN

Shearsman Books Ltd Registered Office
30–31 St. James Place, Mangotsfield, Bristol BS16 9JB
(this address not for correspondence)

www.shearsman.com

ISBN 978-1-84861-946-3

ACKNOWLEDGEMENTS
Most of these poems first appeared in the following chapbooks:
Given (Sava Books), *These* (Granite Press), *No Preference* (Long-house), *Hourglass* (Longhouse), *Prague, etc.* (Kater Murr's Press) and *Included* (Otata). Also, in the following magazines: *Dispatches from the Poetry Wars, Shearsman, Noon (Journal of the Short Poem), Damn the Caesars, Stride, International Times, Half Day Moon Journal* and *Lilliput*. Lastly, in the following anthologies: *"Americans and Others" Anthology* (Camion Press), *Noon: An Anthology of the Short Poems* (Isobar Press), *Modern Haiku 2021* (Modern Haiku Press), and in the book *Language Is*. Sometimes the poems are not the same.

Gratitude to Bob Arnold, Joseph Salvatore Aversano, Michael Boughn, Tony Frazer, Lee Gurga, Kent Johnson, Rupert Loydell, John Martone, Scott Metz, David Miller, Richard Owens, Philip Rowland, Roger Snell, Giulio Tedeschi and Don Wentworth for finding space to give the poems air.

Certain poems are from collaborations with John Levy and James Stallard in which we responded to each other's words.

CONTENTS

In memory of
Kent Johnson
Clive Faust
Graham Jelbert
Theodore Enslin
Gael Turnbull
Cid Corman

& for Lana, Eva and Jasna

& James Stallard

NO PREFERENCE
for Jasper Johns

Sometimes I think it, and then write it
Sometimes I write it, then think it
Sometimes it writes itself, then thinks me
Sometimes it thinks itself, then writes me
Sometimes neither it or me thinks or writes

Each of these situations is impure

EXACTLY

As if there were
someone saying
these words
for someone

else to hear them
being said —
to make sense of
the act of saying,

the act of hearing —
or being here
doing either
As if words could

SEEN
for Eva

crows above a field
will always be
Van Gogh's

TOLD

Tell me a story,
the words say

to no one there
listening. It's

themselves they
want to be told,

themselves they
want to hear.

The only thing
a story tells

is words happening
to be told.

Sometimes
the room we're in is
inside another room
there's no way
to enter. This is the room
in which everything
happens to us,
even if we're elsewhere
when it happens,
which we often are.
Outside this room,
nothing is real.

Of this
silence

I can
tell you

nothing
it can't

say for
itself

UNFINISHED

Each time I say a word
I hear a rustling at the edge
of light
as if something invisible would be-
come tangible
the next instant
that never will

WON'T

Because we are, we know we won't be
and to live is to live for
something other than that

(Which won't be)

THE POINT

Why add more
words to the
too many there
already no one
pays much
attention to or
acts differently
after reading
as if the point of
it all were acting
differently which
hopelessly it is

OLD MASTER

By looking at looking
itself

paint
permits us to see

TREACHERY

What keeps me
coming here

is my wanting
not to

be here at all,
as if cleansing

myself of
words

would permit
silence to

welcome me
back again —

impossibly
uncompromised

RECOGNITION

When these words
are yours
spoken through
this breath
we are shared

REPLY

This poem isn't written
until you finish
                    reading it

SPEECH

My tongue
sewn into
the fabric
of silence

PRAGUE
for Naomi Frears

The painting was titled *Prague*, the city where the artist spent her honeymoon. In the centre, a white metal bed and the head of a young man. Behind the man's head, the erased image of a tree. Two small, delicate impressions of branches – one at the top of the painting, one on the bottom left. The ghost of grid lines over-or-underlay the rest.

For the artist, the bed was an erotic symbol. Jasna and I thought it the bed where Gregor Samsa awoke. The head reminded us of Kafka.

She told us the pencilling of transparent grids was a substitute for her desire to smoke. Sartre said when he lit a cigarette he imagined he was destroying the world.

Jasna noticed the man had no lips. She said this deepened his silence. I thought the silence coiled around a scream.

After we'd hung the painting above the fire, she curled up in her thin dress on the metal bed, hugged her knees and wept.

THIS

Ask
yourself

what you want
from this.

Then give it.

listened to birds are listening

Thinking wonders
what it is

to be unthought
and still there

AFTER BUSON'S PAINTING

for Jonathan Greene

Three crows on
a pine bough

squawking after
another
crow

      not there

ISSA
for Malcolm Ritchie

irksome

mosquitoes

consoling

even

so

Nothing to
do doesn't
stop it
happening

Like no where
to go doesn't
mean we aren't
there

Flies
break

silence

into
    time

ALTERNATING CURRENT

When you're not there
what happens
to you is

repeated later,

somewhat changed

SUCH
for John Martone

What's unseen

is still

to be

recognised as

Nothing is here
before I say
            it is

HERE

Language you
live in

this silence
because I

need you to
say to

whoever is
listening

nothing said
is enough to

make sense
of what will

or will not
happen yet

your failure
is mine

unless
neither of

us end
being treacherous

which is
unlikely

HOPELESS

There is no hope. There never was.
Or if there was, it was a thing

not quite hope which used its name.

Not that it's hopeless. Not yet.
Though, of course, it always is.

THIS

What purpose
in what
has none

That one fact
meant to
be found

NO ONE
for David Miller

The stories we tell ourselves are stories we need to hear
without which we'd forget silence
is necessary for us
to recognise who we mean to be

STONE

Memory is a sea
the drowned
forget to
know

DISPENSATION

History begins
when loss is
saying what
no one present
understands
this going
towards when
& where
no tense
makes sense

UNWRITTEN
for Richard Owens

The letter said everything he possessed would be taken from him. Everything was taken. Later, I find it

held in my hand. Everything is taken from me. The letter I left for you.

SIGNATURE

What we read
we write
ourselves
into
the text of

WHICH HAPPENS
for Liam Hughes

Wittgenstein wrote, 'In philosophy the winner of the race is
the one who runs the most slowly. Or: who gets there last.'

I misread this as saying: Who gets there lost.

I prefer that.

To arrive at the destination
not knowing where you are

or why.

WEATHERING
for Eugène Guillevic

I'm here
doing nothing

What
about you?

PRELUDE
for Cid Corman

You might be asking yourself,
what's the point of this?
What's going to happen?
There are a few faces, some you
recognise, enough to say
the time of day
before the show begins. Not that
it's a show, exactly. Oh,
there's a stage, or what
passes for a stage,
but it remains all but empty.
All that happens is someone
will stand in front of you
reading out words
written earlier
in an unnamed place
some distance away.
Listening, it would be natural
to wonder why. Yet,
of all things, it must've been words
you were expecting. Not
these words. But words.
Hopefully arranged in patterns
of sound & sense
to satisfy the need you came
to fulfil:
           Nothing
as profound
as telling you the reason

you're here. *Here* meaning
the world at large — this
being alive in the first place. Words
can't do that. At least,
not these words.
                    Tell the truth:
You never expected them to.
That wasn't
why you came.
                    If that's what
you're after, you'll have to
make the words up yourself.

CONVERSATION WITH MIROSLAV HOLUB

for Roger Snell

Some say they are poets
because they write poems
some say they're poets
only when writing poems
(not before/not after)
some say a poet is
when others say so
some say why pay attention
to whoever calls themselves a poet
some say everyone's a poet whether they write or not
some don't mention poets or poems

THE CASE

What language
says we
overhear

to think
is us
meaning

TRUCE

Each word keeps saying
another thing

than it said last time
I used it

making me think
what I can trust a word

to say is
that I don't want it to

unless I want it to mean
what I don't say

which might be what's
happening here

THE LABOURS
for Bob Arnold

What silence wants
words
never are
capable of

Still we listen
to fail
to hear it
being said

VIRTUE
for Clive Faust

The words at the end of silence
know nothing we say
will matter the way
our silence will matter if we don't

CORRESPONDENCE

for Eve Luckring

Wallace Stevens was woken
by a cat walking
delicately
on crusted snow

Each least sound, he thought

SIX

Lana asked
if cats
knew they
were animals

did they have
a language
to know
it in

Or did they
think we were
animals
wondering

if we had a
language
to know
ourselves

PLAGIARISM
for Kent Johnson

Writing doesn't belong to
One's is as much another's

THE DESTINY OF
for Wisława Szymborska

What's the fate of a poem?

To be endlessly dissected

recited by a grave in the rain

or slipped into a bottle & tossed into the sea

To be thrown in the waste

burnt ceremoniously by law makers

or be left
unwritten

To be turned into propaganda,
an emperor's whore

or to be forgotten

discovered in an ancient anthology
under *Anonymous*

To be misunderstood

trampled on

or traced onto the breasts of a beloved
with a tongue of dancing light

INDEX

Every poet is
anonymous

Nothing was
said by them

UNGARETTI

Lit with illumination am I

When libraries burn   eat weeds

THE CREATION OF BEAUTY
for & from
Mahmoud Darwish & Yehuda Amichai

I

Sometimes I want to
go back and forget

the letters of the alphabet.
I am tired of

my intractable hope,
tired like a room

in a hotel.
Behind my words,

dark as a moon,
the dove builds her nest

in an iron helmet. The soldiers
pitched their camp

in a faraway place and
she knows about

the resurrection of
the dead man

as he lies in her arms.

And he says:
I am not a citizen

and the prophets
died long ago.

One day I'll become
what I want,

not the peace
of a cease-fire.

II

Here strangers
hang rifles

on olive branches,
in each of their heads

a single thought.

In the morning a wind
comes up from the sea,

blows through
the empty chairs.

I pass the house
where I was born

only to bid farewell
to what was

hidden within me.

As in a child's game,
he was lying

dead on a stone.
A girl by the spring

fills her water jug and
every night

the memory
of the garden.

Both of us blind,
searching for

a god or a son.

III

In another country,
on a bridge,

he said to me: They
killed the little girl

from my childhood
and my father is dead.

I have to live now
until every number

is sacred,
then forget them all

to remember
the victim

behind the curtain.
With the silent

closing of a door,
your daughter

becomes a widow.
The remembrance

of a journey in rain.
Like a full cemetery,

I waited for no one.

Once I loved,
then died,

awoke
on the grass

of my grave
believing it was

all a mistake.
Perhaps my entire life.

IV

We measure the distance
between each body

and all my memories
are closed courtyards.

The detainee told
the interrogator:

My heart is filled.
I see the children

playing in the sand.
I saw them on the road

to the well
before my birth.

Nothing disappears
in this world.

On a bed of dew
a bird now,

instead of us.

I wash my hands
before the mirror

and know one is
a murderer if he

witnesses a murder
and says nothing.

V

You can't go back
to anything,

but the perfect mistake
makes a perfect life.

And because of the war

a young man
marries a girl

but they have no place
for their wedding night.

I open an iron door
over which is written:

All that happened
never happened.

The almond tree
is in bloom.

What crime did I
commit to make you

destroy me?
Whenever I wake up

strange things
happen, yet

the author is not I.

VI

Back then we didn't know

what they were
teaching, but soon

we learnt: Here or
there, our blood

will plant olive trees.

He said: I'm obsessed
with a reality

I cannot decipher.

When you journey and
can't find the dream,

touch each other
at dusk between

the legs. And only
after my death

will you learn I am
yours as your hand

is yours. And I was
lying on top of you,

heavy and quiet,
snow falling

on the mountains.

But in my heart,
where I live,

I have not withdrawn
from the world.

VII

Because of love
and because of

making love, I asked:
Is the impossible

far away? But at dusk,
in the thin rain,

a cafe, and you with
the newspaper, laughing.

If I could speak to
the women on the road,

I'd say: They did
what they had to do,

and drowned near
the shore.

And I ask one thing —
let your mouth touch

mine one time
before you deny me.

I have nothing to say

about the war, nothing —
and don't want a country.

Like dogs, drawn by
the smell, he said,

we will live, even if
life abandons us.

VIII

She stopped me
in the street:

If you dare to speak,
you must take action.

Everything is true.

There is no answer.

In foreign cities
I rent hotel rooms

to desire or disappear.

As fate would have it,

she is naked
and not alone.

Everything begins to
resemble everything else:

Like words, like flies.

Or maybe I died before.
Don't promise anything

and forgive me
for what I didn't do.

IX

'I wish I never loved you,'
includes the pain

of all that did not happen.
But the night disappears

into the night where I
waited years ago,

when I was a little boy.
I have the wisdom of one

condemned to death
for things I don't know.

Sometimes a whole life
passes: Don't let that happen.

Repeat the words again:
Perhaps she has come

to love you. And other words
like these: How far is far?

Or the mystery of
words like:

No more, no less.

X

This land is less
than the blood

of its offspring.

If it were up to me
to bring back

the beginning,
I would.

Words are simple.

I know that I know
how to kill.

Still we celebrate,

punctuating time
with the same

ancient machine.
Whenever I think

about the woman
and the garden,

I want to return.
At night I walk again

along the row of
empty willows — no one

behind me; no one
ahead.

But what's the meaning
of this?

We talk a great deal
about death.

The soldiers in the grave
say: You, up there.

What do you want?

XI

And as if nothing
has happened,

war still pretends
to be peace.

This is the situation.
Do not forget

the people of the camps.
Most of our lives

we are bound
to the dead

who remember
nothing.

This is the wound.

Words haunt me.
They haunt my life.

Here they killed me.

A bomb exploded
in the language of longing.

I still remember
what it said: Nothing is

left of me except you.

XII

A woman once told me:
I know this story.

We bear the pain
all our lives. It's

the lightness of
the eternal

in the everyday.
I don't know what words

make them happy.
For me it's essential

to reject death.

She slipped off her dress
and a legacy of chains.

The train went swiftly by
and suddenly I wept,

because of so much.

On this evening I
think again:

If you were another,
if I were.

XIII

I hear footsteps in the dark,

of insomnia
and eternity,

of a woman I loved.

I said: Are you talking
to yourself or to me?

I cannot help you.

After making love
we stood once more by the sea.

The war had ended.

What else was I
supposed to do?

I was neither
dead nor alive.

Words begin to
abandon me...

They gagged his mouth.

CODA

Old friend —
which of us

died
before the other

STONE

If you insist on being here
at least say something

PORTAL

Silence in the hand
is a bird
in a mouth
of leaves

WINDOWS
for John Levy

My words don't have to be thinking what I am, unless they say what they're thinking to me. If they keep their thoughts to themselves, what they think is invisible. Sometimes the moon is invisible. The distance between my thoughts and the words which shape my thoughts might be the same as between the moon and myself. I can't calculate where to begin and my words refuse to. In the sunlight, in the moonlight, distance is different. There are buildings without windows from which to see the moon. Some thoughts are windows.

Light needs
no name

to hear
sight say

UNSAID

This says every
thing there is
for it to say
which isn't this

THIS

The act is self-
definition

in the act of
self-denial —

penetrating
what is not there

to fail to get
through into you

THIS

How it is
given to be

taken away
from never

having hold
of that most

precious
long enough

to know it
is over

THIS
for Nelson Ball

There is
a here

we aren't
close to

even if
it's where

we are

AFTER CREELEY

In back of car

being driven
by another

you can't see
to a destination

neither
will reach

INSCRIBED
for Graham Jelbert

Forgiving the dead's not easy
Even their dreams are gone
Don't think they think of us
Or care one way or another

Every moment
is
where it's
      never
      been
returning
to
where it
      never
      was

CONVERGENCE
for Octavio Paz

Endless
the arrival

you are
going from

AT

Why not
let it rain

Where's to go
I am

HONEY

for Jasna

Poetry is an instance of attention given to a seemingly unimportant occurrence: the setting of word against word, each weighed within silence. So much being done through carelessness or not caring, poetry achieves — against its will — a use money can't buy: akin to breathing well. Or remembering when my daughter was born, the crown of her head smelled of honey.

UNQUENCHABLE
for Andrew Schelling

One moment a child
the next
belly full
the stink of death
threw me to
money
mockery and sin
a dog
craving truth
I died for nothing
in the blink of
an eye

ONE

Each leaf
suggests
another

even if
there is

PLURAL

Someone else
might not
      think
this
   this way
even if
     this is
what
    they think

What shapes
silence
      makes us
become
      to each
other
    words
invent
    to say
we mean more
than not
      saying so

SHADE

If we resemble
meaning

it's only

the shadow
a light

casts

we are blind
to see

SLANT

through
 rain
sieved
light

 silence
slurs

SPELL

Listen
carefully

you may
hear a word

in the silence
thinking

to say
something not

said before

to make something
happen

that hasn't
happened before

one word
with the belief

changing silence
changes everything

GIVEN

the shape of
the unseen
      in the shape of
      the seen

ENVOI

What death writes
we all
end up
reading

SPIRAL
for Theodore Enslin

'the sense of
loss
your going
makes'

the sense your
going
makes
of loss

AMEN

Today I met my father
in the street.

After all these years,
he was still dead.

I could feel his heart
beat in my chest.

The heart wasn't mine.
It belonged to his son.

Who I no longer was.

IDENTITY

No, I was never there.

That was someone else
who recalls
meeting you
in a place
neither of us
ever visited.

Remember?

STANZA
for Fred Jeremy Seligson

It's not even certain
this is a room

we're in: it could be
a poem and who I take

to be myself merely
the words saying it.

The fact you are here
makes the room

more likely than if I

were alone. But if the room
were a poem it

would demand another to
hear itself being said.

Perhaps the room is a poem
whose words we are

and whoever speaks is

opening a door into
another room that may be

darkened or lit depending
on what the words mean.

Perhaps a poem is a room
in the dream of a word.

TAIGI
for Gael Turnbull

what else

quick

so

but

swallows

ENVOI
for James Stallard

Time I read
            a few poems
looking out over
                  the hills
before
      the mosquitoes
      come

Sitting here
              not noticing
              it's raining
              until
      it stops

HOURGLASS

Slipping through
my fingers

time is sand
in my shoes

PRACTICE

I sit for hours

facing nothing

no word
to witness

the silence

my mind
refuses

is prayer

Milton Keynes UK
Ingram Content Group UK Ltd.
UKHW031525290824
447545UK00006B/167